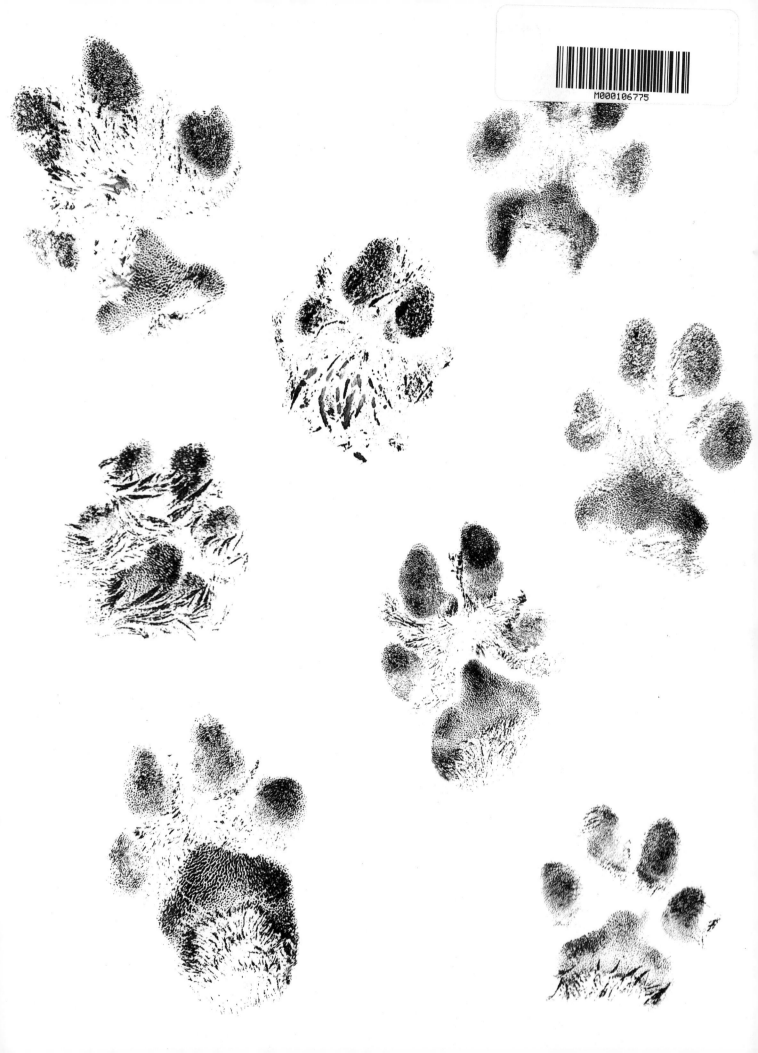

At Home with Dogs

RESCUE LOVE STORIES

At Home with Dogs

RESCUE LOVE STORIES

NATALIA KING-SUN AND
PATRICIA HART MCMILLAN

SCHIFFER PUBLISHING

4880 Lower Valley Road • Atglen, PA 19310

Library of Congress Control Number: 2020930877

Cover and interior design by Ashley Millhouse
All photos by Natalia King-Sun unless otherwise noted
Type set in Bitstream Vera Serif/Bitstream Vera Sans
ISBN: 978-0-7643-6046-6
Printed in China

Published by Schiffer Publishing, Ltd.
4880 Lower Valley Road
Atglen, PA 19310
Phone: (610) 593-1777; Fax: (610) 593-2002
E-mail: Info@schifferbooks.com
Web: www.schifferbooks.com

For our complete selection of fine books on this and related subjects, please visit our website at www.schifferbooks.com. You may also write for a free catalog.

Schiffer Publishing's titles are available at special discounts for bulk purchases for sales promotions or premiums. Special editions, including personalized covers, corporate imprints, and excerpts, can be created in large quantities for special needs. For more information, contact the publisher.

We are always looking for people to write books on new and related subjects. If you have an idea for a book, please contact us at proposals@schifferbooks.com.

Other Schiffer Books by Patricia Hart McMillan:
Christmas at Designers' Homes across America, ISBN 978-0-7643-5163-1
Sí, San Antonio: Our Favorite Places, People, and Things at Christmas, ISBN 978-0-7643-6093-0

Other Schiffer Books on Related Subjects:
Senior Dogs Across America, Nancy LeVine, ISBN 978-0-7643-5111-2

To Precious, my first dog, whom I loved dearly

—Natalia

Remembering TajMa, Old Ring, Reelfoot, Sam, and Doug

—Patricia

OUR GRATITUDE

Pete Schiffer, our enthusiastic publisher

Cheryl Weber, our encouraging editor

Peggy Story Brink and CARE for incredible support

Homeowners who became rescuers

The amazing dogs who found forever homes

Contents

So Much Love

When John and I adopted Jasper—then named Ruben—in the summer of 2009 from the SPCA of Westchester, New York, we had never owned a dog. In fact, John was a bit hesitant, having once been chased and bitten as a child. But we had a feeling that a dog would add something wonderful and unexpected to our lives, so we browsed online and found a charming Boston-boxer mix up for adoption.

Why a Boston? John and I felt an affinity for the breed. Something spoke to us about the soulful eyes and compact body. And we definitely wanted a pound rescue.

We were living in Brooklyn, so we piled into the car and drove upstate to meet the little guy after being approved for adoption. We were instantly smitten. Big, big ears. One blue eye. Ruben was a little slobbery, but so what? John forgot his fear of dogs on the spot. We finished up the paperwork and trundled Jasper into the car and home.

The rest, as they say, is history.

Jasper was our entry into a brand-new, magical world of pound-rescue parenting. The 25-pound pup has sat in our laps in the front seat on myriad road trips. He has scampered around the fields surrounding our weekend getaway in the Catskill Mountains. He has watched TV with us and always picks the choicest pillows to sit on. He has sat on John's lap as John designed interiors and products at the computer. He has given us endless kisses and followed us everywhere.

Eventually, Jasper was joined by three—yes, three!—pound-rescue pugs—Weenie, Amy Petunia, and Cecil. He welcomed them with open paws and graciously shared his kingdom. What a terrific little family we had. Jasper was team leader, and the pugs looked up to him for guidance. The pug trio did everything he did.

Jasper always seemed so happy and thankful to have been adopted. Sadly, after ten incredible years together that took us from New York to North Carolina, the always-vital Jasper suddenly developed seizures and, after a few weeks of endless vet appointments and sleepless nights and heaps of worry, passed away in our arms at home early on a Saturday morning. John and I were devastated.

We have taken lots of time to celebrate Jasper's memory and now move forward while remembering many life lessons that he indirectly taught us. We are so thankful that this little pound-rescue tyke came into our lives. He reminds us to take stock and enjoy every day. And not to worry about the small things.

So much love in such a little package with such big, big ears.

—*Jason Oliver Nixon, Madcap Cottage*

Photo courtesy Madcap Cottage

Rescuing Love

No creature showers us with such unconditional love, trust, and forgiveness as a rescue dog.

I witness love every day. I see it in the eyes of those who adopt rescues when they come face to face with *their* dog. I see it reflected in the face of the dog who somehow knows that *their* human has arrived—at last! My own dogs inspire me every day to be my best self and treat animals with the respect, dignity, and love they deserve. Indeed, the love I felt for my dog, Cressie, inspired me to begin CARE (Cressie Animal Refuge and Enrichment), a rescue and adoption agency.

Ten years ago the euthanizing of smart, able dogs was not a part of my daily awareness. Today it is! It's startling to realize that more than a million dogs a year are euthanized in shelters across the US. That knowledge has driven me to be part of a movement to enlighten everyone on the blessings of adopting a rescue dog. The chapter "Ginger and Cheddar, At home with Al and Jo Schmidt," tells of my saving Cheddar from euthanasia and Al's extraordinary effort to adopt this wonderful creature.

The stories shared here reflect the joy that dogs bring to our lives. They also make clear the simple fact that rescuing a shelter dog is not always a cakewalk! It takes a special person to accept the task of undoing the harm that has often been done to these innocent creatures. But every rescuer tells me that the reward for their effort is priceless. I am grateful that I and CARE have had the opportunity to match these precious pets with loving families.

A special thank you to authors Patricia Hart McMillan and Natalia King-Sun, who thought there should be a book about rescue love stories. Natalia's portraits capture the love and happiness of these amazing creatures. We hope this book will encourage more adoptions.

—*Peggy Story Brink, CARE Founder*

Photographing Love

It has been a joy to photograph fifteen amazing dogs for this book. Growing up, I never had a dog; however, I had a few animal friends: my grandmother's cow, Buryonka, who always smelled like fresh milk; my cat, Mashka, who let me build elaborate cardboard houses and stuff her in there; a hedgehog, Grisha, who turned into a prickly ball every time I tried to pet him; and a random bird with a broken wing who flew away when I nursed her back to life. I have always loved my animals.

In my adult life I finally became a "dog person." My son got a pug named Precious for his birthday. She spent her first few hours in our home running through rooms at a hundred miles per hour, chasing invisible happiness, having found her new family. Precious became my first animal subject to photograph. At the time, I did it just for fun. She passed away suddenly four years later, and having those photographs of her warms my heart and keeps a beautiful memory alive.

Years later, I became a commercial photographer. However, I couldn't resist photographing animals. I started hosting annual dog portrait marathons in my studio, with dogs lined up outside the door for picture day. It felt good to gain the trust of the furry creatures in front of my lens and capture that special spark in their eyes, often not without the help of a "dog whisperer" friend on set. The rewards for being a pet photographer were a lick on the hand, an occasional wink, and the wag of a fluffy tail. Photographing animals taught me to seize the moment, practice patience, and trust the subject for its own original way of self expression.

Today I live with a family of six rescue dogs: the smartest chiweenie in the world, THX; two unruly chihuahuas, Godzilla and Trex; a loving rat terrier mix, Marbles; a constantly kissing dwarf black Labrador, Lilly; and a vocal, singing Doberman, Ali. Every day is a new adventure with them—and sometimes a challenge. They are always grateful, not asking for anything in return, and teaching me how to be a better human.

In today's hyperactive world, we often become overwhelmed and lose sense of our identity. Through caring for an animal, spending time with our pets, giving and receiving unconditional love, we find a cure for ourselves. Dogs are healers for our hearts and souls; they bring us simple joy of life; they teach us lessons of forgiving; they ground us in a sense that no other remedy could. I hope my photographs of the families and their rescues capture that sentiment. And I hope this book will inspire people to build their own magical connections with pets and reach out in their community to help animals in need.

—Natalia King-Sun, www.nataliasun.com, San Antonio

Marcus

AT HOME WITH MARY FURGUSON AND MIKE WISH

San Antonio, Texas

We met Marcus at a CARE function at the Pearl, the historic San Antonio Pearl Brewery repurposed as elegant apartments, shops, and restaurants. He was friendly and sweet, and we decided to adopt him. On a Saturday about two weeks later, we met up with Marcus's foster keeper, who handed him over in tears. Marcus cried all the way home too.

At first Marcus was well-behaved, like his new siblings Zoe, Zeke, and Bella—low-key toy poodles. Then came wild behavior, and we were at the vet's often. Marcus was nocturnal and a runner. We had chicken wire put around the fence and still he escaped. The neighbors saw me in all types of outfits running after Marcus, After about two weeks, we called Invisible Fence. Marcus may have had the desire to run, but we had it under control.

For the first six months he would sit politely at the dining table while we ate. Mike called him "Manners the Butler." But one night he jumped up from the seat and grabbed a steak. He still steals occasionally if we are not looking, and he loves a cookie. He also loves slippers. He takes mine into the yard, so I'm always minus one.

Marcus is a ball-playing fool. His main love is a tennis ball. Anyone who comes to the house is another player in the game. He has endless energy and can play for a very long time. Sometimes he runs on the driveway full force with his ball in his mouth. I can only imagine the friction this causes on his pads. The neighborhood kids squeal with delight when Marcus dives into the pool. We call it cooling his toes. He loves the pool, and sometimes he and Mike play "dive rockets" from the first step.

ADOPTION
TIP

Remember that the owner is the alpha
or leader who shows the beta dog
approval and affection. When the dog
feels that love has been earned and
asks for it, show it! (The alpha leader
does not ask for affection, but gives it.)

Marcus • poodle/Maltese mix • 10 years

Marcus is a ball-playing fool.
His main love is a tennis ball.
Anyone who comes to the house
is another player in the game.

Marcus has never met anyone he didn't like. He meets visitors at the door with a toy in his mouth and loves our grandchildren, Delyn and Clayton. When they visit, they like to put him in the dollhouse baby bed and "feed" him plastic food from the playhouse kitchen. Marcus is happy to play along. Once when we were at their house, granddaughter Adelyn kidnapped Marcus, took him to her room, put him in a dollhouse horse barn, and covered him with baby blankets. We could not find him! For once, he couldn't escape.

While our other three dogs like to pack themselves into the utility room, Marcus has his own chair in the study. We had it reupholstered recently, and when the upholsterers left with *his* chair, Marcus tried to leave with them. He is the most grateful dog. I think he has a full understanding of where he came from. He hates cold weather, and I hate to think about where he was and how he was treated during his first year. Now he has his own study and loads of toys and balls—his own Neverland.

There are days when I curse his nonstop energy. But then I look into those soulful brown eyes. He gets out of a lot of trouble by making "sweet eyes" and flashing his crooked smile. He's a real charmer. We are ever so grateful to Peggy Story Brink for saving Marcus.

—*Mary Furguson*

MATCHMAKING
TIP

Mary and Mike needed a
hypoallergenic dog that
would fit in with their pack.
Shih tzu, schnauzer, bichon
frise, and poodles are
considered hypoallergenic,
among other breeds.

—Peggy Story Brink

Sir Freckles

AT HOME WITH PAUL AND SILVIA ALLEN

San Antonio, Texas

We lost our two golden retrievers when they were seven and eight years old. The loss was absolutely heartbreaking, and we didn't know if we could ever bring another dog into our lives. But we did. Adopting Freckles has been one of the most rewarding experiences for our family.

We first met Freckles at his foster home after CARE pulled him from the animal shelter. Paul named him Freckles because of all the cute freckles all over his paws and face. We teased that it wasn't a very masculine name, so his status was elevated to Sir Freckles.

Before we could bring him home, he had to undergo an intense three-day treatment for severe heart worm. He got very sick from the medicaton's side effects and suffered permanent kidney damage. It's a shame that people ignore heartworm prevention—the disease is 100-percent avoidable.

When we brought Freckles home, he didn't want anything to do with us. He was extremely anxious, had a lot of nervous energy, and refused to eat. At that time we were working out of our home, with strangers coming and going all day. He was scared and unsettled for a while and even tried to run away a couple of times. Having a dog that didn't seem to want us was strange, but we tried to give him a lot of space and love. Time and patience has turned him into a little love bug, and now he is attached to us.

In fact, at one point Freckles developed a nearly uncontrollable case of separation anxiety. He became destructive when left alone, which was a problem because he didn't take well to crate training. (Who hasn't seen John Grogan's book and movie *Marley and Me?*) Our vet suggested professional training and anxiety medication.

ADOPTION
TIP

Commit! Many rescue dogs have been
traumatized, neglected, or physically
abused. Before you adopt, consider
grooming expenses and medical bills,
which can get costly. Make sure you
are in it for the dog's lifetime.

Those interventions solved the anxiety problem, but we still couldn't get Freckles to eat. He sensed our concern and looked so sad at feeding time; he really wanted to please. We found that although the problem was related to severe chronic back pain, it was solved with home-cooked meals. I guess we required some training as well! We feed him meals of brown rice, chicken breast, carrots, sweet potato, peas, pumpkin, and coconut oil.

Freckles doesn't like to play with people, toys, or other dogs. I strongly believe that, like humans, dogs need to have a sense of purpose. He contributes by being a friendly greeter at the office and by "taking out the trash" at home. Obviously he can't hold the bag, but he goes through the motions. It's his job, and it makes him feel important. Dogs are not so different from people in that they want to be loved, appreciated, respected, and cared for. It's really not very complicated.

—Silvia Allen

Sir Freckles • golden retriever/spaniel mix • 10 or 11 years old

Dogs are not so different from people in that they want to be loved, appreciated, respected, and cared for. It's really not very complicated.

MATCHMAKING
TIP

A rough start in life leaves many
shelter dogs with serious health
issues. Freckles would need
regular, costly vet visits. Silvia and
Paul could handle the financial
demands and would treat with love
and patience Sir Freckles' health
challenges. The match was made.

—*Peggy Story Brink*

44

Chloe

AT HOME WITH SHARI HARBINGER AND JEFF STEIN
New York City

As I was roaming the internet and landed on Petfinder, a beautiful white terrier named Darcy popped up. I quickly realized she was from a Texas shelter and didn't understand how I had landed on this rescue site using a New York City filter, but it didn't matter. We would go anywhere to get our dog, and this particular puppy fit our wish list. After contacting the rescue group, I received a response from Emily Cleveland, who forwarded my request to the foster mom. I had a good feeling about her and this rescue group.

Unfortunately, Darcy needed a dog companion, and we were told she was to be placed in another home. We were bummed. But Emily promised to continue looking for us. We found another puppy we were interested in, but the application process took so long that by the time they contacted us, I had already received an email from Emily with pictures of a sweet and scruffy black terrier named Chloe. I had been on the train on my way home from work and emailed Emily back, begging her not to show the dog to anyone else until I showed Jeff. She assured me that she felt the same way and believed this was the puppy we were searching for.

The foster mom sent us some videos of Chloe in action. We had waited a long time for our work and life balance to be aligned so that we could spend quality time with a dog. We planned to travel, go out on our boat, go to the beach, run in the sand, and go swimming, and we wanted a dog that could do these things with us. We knew the moment we saw the action videos that Chloe had to be ours. We just hoped and prayed that the foster mom would feel the same way. On a phone call with her the next day, we had a lovely chat, and thankfully, we were approved. A week later we met our puppy at LaGuardia airport.

We were overjoyed! Our first impression was how sweet, brave, and resilient she was! She looked so cute in that crate, but I couldn't wait to open the door and welcome her to her new home and into our arms. Ours was an instant love affair with lots of kisses—oh, does Chloe love to kiss. This dog made getting acquainted easy. She just wanted to be loved and held, and that's all we wanted to do with her. You could say it was a match made in heaven. She was a cuddle bug from the minute we opened the crate. She sat calmly in our arms the entire taxi ride into Manhattan.

Chloe seemed happy, generous, needy, and relieved. On day three, as she became more comfortable with us and her new surroundings, we saw a feistier side appear. She is a combination of calm and feisty at any given moment.

Chloe didn't know her name at first, but she learned quickly. Within a day she was responding to her name along with fundamental commands such as sit, stay, come, and no. And she was doing her business outside like a champ. She is expressive and communicative. The learning curve was on us and our ability to understand her signals. She had two accidents, which were our fault. Now we know the sounds and behaviors that indicate her needs. I began to research and try some basic training techniques, and we signed her up for puppy training.

Shortly after arriving, Chloe developed a short-lived kennel cough. It was sad to see her uncomfortable, so we brought her into our bed and she nuzzled into us. It felt as if she was telling us she was sad, didn't know what was happening, and needed us. When she needs to release energy, she goes crazy, running all over the house or battling with a toy. She makes adorable grunting sounds to let us know she's in charge, even though she isn't—or is she?

We are still in the adjustment period. Chloe is not yet ready to roam around the apartment unattended. But she loves her crate. We put an anti-anxiety doll with a beating heart in the crate, and she loves it. She doesn't make a peep at night. When we wake up, we bring her into the bed for a few minutes. It is a delicious moment and a great way to start the day.

She's learning to be a watchdog. When she hears people in the hallway, she barks and growls, which is really cute coming from an eleven-pound puppy. On walks, she is a bit skittish with all the activity and noise. She still needs her second round of shots, so we can't really take her out in public yet, but she loves going in the car. We are happy about that, because we plan to travel with her a lot.

—Shari Harbinger

ADOPTION
TIP

Choosing the right animal is a gut feeling. Don't ignore those feelings. Be ready to take on a rescue puppy with all its medical needs. Ask many questions about its past, get the medical papers, and get your puppy to a vet immediately to get a baseline checkup. At this young age, puppies are still building their immune systems. Do not let your puppy mingle with other dogs until your vet gives you the thumbs up.

Chloe • terrier mix • 5 months old

Ours was an instant love affair with lots of kisses— oh, does Chloe love to kiss.

MATCHMAKING
TIP

Shari and Jeff asked for a
small, active adult dog to
match their energy level, one
that would comfortably meet
new people and adjust well to
the noise and bustle of New
York City. Chloe was the
perfect answer to that tall
order.

—*Peggy Story Brink*

Pepper

AT HOME WITH JEFF, CATHY, ELLA, AND ISAAK FRIIS-ALFERS
Seattle, Washington

We were struck by Pepper's unusual markings and silky coat. Other people are drawn to him, too. Sometimes we make bets on how many people will comment as they walk by: *Oh my gosh, did you see that dog's blaze on his eye*? *That dog is so cute*! *Look at that dog—he totally prances when he walks!* Pepper came to us with the name River, but we thought he needed a "peppier" name. One of our friends uses white pepper in a lot of her recipes, and we thought, "That is it! *White* Pepper! And it stuck.

We had been fostering Pepper while looking for a companion to our older dog, Ollie. We noticed how devoted Pepper was to Ollie. They slept in the same dog bed, and Pepper was like Ollie's shadow. Since they were so compatible, we asked if we could adopt him. Karen, a CARE-Tx volunteer, came to our house to talk and watch the dogs play. We keep in contact with Karen to this day.

We had been told about Pepper's separation anxiety, which made the getting-acquainted period a bit rocky. Every time we left him alone in the house, he would do his business in the same place. We laughed when we read that if you put their food bowl in the spot where they have gone potty, they won't go there anymore. We put the bowl there, and then discovered that he had relieved himself *in the bowl*—perfect aim, apparently. But that lasted only a few weeks. He relaxed after he realized that we were his forever home and would always come back to him. Now he always tells us when he needs to go outside.

At first, Pepper was quite submissive and would stand behind Ollie, an alpha female. They were good with each other. Pepper needed a doting mother; Ollie needed a purpose again. She had raised our two human kids, Ella and Isaak, and kept them safe. Now she needed another project. Lovingly and patiently, Ollie raised Pepper, who was depressed for about a month after Ollie passed away. Even today, Pepper respects his place in the pack. He's

ADOPTION
TIP

Go in with a whole heart.
Understand what you are getting
into. Clear time on your schedule—
the effort you put into your pet will
have a much larger reward.

gentle when approaching us for love. He doesn't jump on furniture except for the area we've given him. In many ways, his working-dog traits make him an easy family member.

Over time, Pepper has gained confidence. He started leaving Ollie's side and trusting each of us separately. But after Ollie passed, Pepper would almost seek guidance from us so he knew what he could or couldn't do. He still looks you straight in the eyes to see what your next move will be and is always ready to head to the closet where we keep the leash! He travels with us everywhere and comes when called.

Pepper has beds in the living room, TV room, office, and master bedrom. But at night he sleeps in the master bedroom with a clear view of the stairs outside our door—a watch dog for sure!

Pepper has chosen Jeff (dad) as his "person," but he gives each of us love every day. After Ollie passed away, Pepper assumed Ollie's spot on the couch, which gives him a clear view of anyone coming up the sidewalk. He barks and growls to let us know when we get deliveries or if another dog walks by the house. He is very informative, and we are happy about that.

Life with Pepper means listening to him sing along (howl) when Ella and Isaak play their clarinets. Isaak knitted a blue collar protector to add to Pepper's clothing collection, which includes a Seahawks jersey, a Halloween costume, and a Christmas sweater. He looks darling in all of them, but I can't say he enjoys wearing them. Pepper likes to play chase and obstacle course. He loves going for walks twice a day and smiles the whole time! His favorite walk is to the beach.

—*Cathy Friis-Alfers*

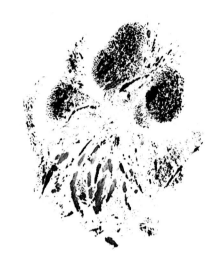

Pepper • mixed rat terrier/white Swiss shepard/Australian cattle dog/Pomeranian • 3 years old

Sometimes we make bets on how many people will comment as they walk by: "Oh my gosh, did you see that dog's blaze on his eye? That dog is so cute! Look at that dog—he totally prances when he walks!"

MATCHMAKING
TIP

Sometimes a dog adopts a
family! When Cathy agreed
to foster a dog that was in
placement transition, Pepper
wiggled her way into Cathy's
heart—the perfect companion
to Cathy's older dog.

—Peggy Story Brink

Ocho

AT HOME WITH GREG, KELSIE, AVERY, AND ELLIE DEVEER
Seattle, Washington

We had to say goodbye to our loyal shepherd mix, Baker, in 2015, after fourteen years. It was a tough loss and took us some time to recover. In the summer of 2017, we felt ready to search for a new pup. We knew we wanted a shepherd mix again. We love their protective demeanor, slick look, and agility. Baker had been a rescue, and we wanted another rescue. We searched all over Washington and Oregon but had difficulty finding the right dog.

I finally posted on Facebook in hopes that social media magic would put us in touch with the right people. It wasn't long until a good friend who had also lost a shepherd mix contacted me about CARE. Things snowballed after that. I filled out an application, explained what we were looking for, and within days we had a call. Hurricane Harvey was rolling into Texas and litters were being surrendered. CARE seemed buried in animals looking for a good home. We heard that a shepherd-mix litter had arrived, and before long we got a picture of our future pup.

Ocho arrived in Seattle on a warm, sunny September day. He had had a long trip in a crate traveling from Texas to Washington. When we heard his cries of excitement, my two little girls started crying, too. We could hardly contain our excitement. We opened the crate and he leapt into my arms and covered my face in puppy kisses. We placed his new collar on him, attached his leash, and took him on his first walk. He was more interested in us than walking. I was worried that he would be scared or anxious after such a big adventure, but it was as if he knew he was coming home. He snuggled between my two daughters during the ride home, perfectly content.

Finding a name was not difficult. During the twenty years my husband and I have been together, we have had many pets. Ocho was our eighth.

With any puppy, the housebreaking and biting can become frustrating. But Ocho was easier than expected. He handled his crate well, slept through the night, and adapted to our cats. A quick learner, he was eager to please—and to get treats!

ADOPTION
TIP

Trust your gut. You never know
what you're going to get, but that's
the best part. Rescue dogs are so
grateful for someone to love and
someone who will love them.

While Baker had been an amazing dog, he didn't play well with others—people or dogs. Ocho is the opposite. He loves the cats, our backyard chickens, and every person and dog he meets. He can hard-core wrestle with a Burmese mountain dog or lie passively while a Yorkie repeatedly jumps on his face.

Ocho wound his way into our hearts. We started out with strict rules: he wouldn't be allowed on the furniture and definitely not on the bed. But before we knew it, he was sleeping at the bottom of our bed. In the morning Ocho helps Greg feed the cats and chickens before he gets his own breakfast.

We like dogs that can be trusted off-leash, and we lucked out with Ocho. When we're out, he stays close, checks in, and constantly circles around us to make sure we stay together. A few weeks after Ocho arrived, we visited the San Juan Islands. Before boarding the ferry, we took him for a long walk to give him an opportunity to relieve himself. He was so overwhelmed with all the activity that he wouldn't "go." Back in the car on the ferry, we rolled the windows down so Ocho could smell the sea air and feel the wind on his face. It was a blissful moment. Everyone was silent when all of a sudden we heard a long and steady stream of water. With his head out the window and his paws on the window sill, he released the longest pee of his life. Laughter filled the car as we scrambled to contain it.

The most endearing thing about Ocho is his eyes, which are the gateway to his soul. We have friends who've paid thousands of dollars for a purebred and spent hours with puppies before choosing the one that fit their family dynamic. And we picked Ocho from a picture! We had no idea what we would get. He's different-looking than we expected and 100 percent better than we imagined.

—*Kelsie deVeer*

Ocho • shepherd/Labrador mix • 1½ years old

We opened the crate and he leapt into my arms and covered my face in puppy kisses. We placed his new collar on him, attached his leash, and took him on his first walk. He was more interested in us than walking.

MATCHMAKING
TIP

Size, breed, and temperament
were important considerations
in matching Ocho to the deVeer
household with young children.
Kelsie and Greg deVeer made
sure that all family members
were in agreement and would
play a supporting role in their
dog's life.

—Peggy Story Brink

Buddy

AT HOME WITH GEOFFREY BURBRIDGE AND DAVIN MULVEY
San Antonio, Texas

Davin and I are foster failures.

Buddy had been living on the street in our neighborhood and would not approach anyone. We understand that. We have two shiba inu dogs, a Japanese breed—Yoshi, seven, and Momo, four. Shibas are the "cats" of dogs—affectionate and attentive on their own terms, but they don't give trust easily. So when we saw the little dog under an RV in our neighbor's driveway Davin went over, sat in the driveway, and tried to coax him out. When he finally did come out, the little dog just rolled into Davin's lap. He seemed excited to have a friend!

At first our intent was to foster this dog through CARE. He was shy and careful, but once he experienced something, he seemed to love it. Naming him was easy. As we integrated him into our home and life, he just seemed like our Buddy. And our temporary home became his permanent home.

Buddy is all love. The most endearing thing about him is the way he gently kisses you while calmly looking into your eyes. He loves to be with us, napping in bed or on the sofa. And loves to play with anything you give him, even a stick. Evening play time after dinner is a ritual.

Buddy eats his food, comes when called, and sleeps like a rock (under our bed—I think it makes him feel safe, like living under the RV). This behavior seems odd to us, because the shibas are so different. It's funny to see him interact with Momo, because he tries to bamboozle her. Occasionally he makes shiba vocalizations (see "shiba scream" on YouTube), which is funny too. Buddy has separation anxiety. When he destroys something while we are away, it makes me sad, because it's important for him to know that we are always going to come home.

—Geoffrey Burbridge and Davin Mulvey

ADOPTION
TIP

Be open. Rescue dogs have experienced things prior to joining you. The challenge is to try to figure out what that was so you can make their living environment as safe and caring as possible. Be patient and consistent.

Buddy • mixed breed • 1 year old

The most endearing thing about him is the way he gently kisses you while calmly looking into your eyes.

MATCHMAKING
TIP

Buddy was a shy and fearful pup.
Geoffrey and Davin offered the
gentle coaxing and understanding
essential to helping him come out of
his shell and become their buddy.

—Peggy Story Brink

Molly

AT HOME WITH TERESA AND RICH TELISKA
San Antonio, Texas

My beautiful chocolate Lab had just been put to sleep. I knew I needed to get a pal for my other dog, Maverick, and also to fill that void in my heart. I reached out to my friend Peggy at CARE, and she sent me photos of pups. I mulled over her hand-picked selection for a couple of days, and then I went to visit Molly. I saw her sweet little face, held out my hand, which she sniffed and licked, and then we went for a little stroll. I found a bench and put her in my lap, and we sat there for a while. Peggy had done a wonderful thing—she had helped me find the perfect pup.

I am terrible at picking out names. First I chose Milly. My son was horrified because his best friend was named Milly. So I named my new pup Molly, which fit her loving nature.

At first Molly was skittish, so I made a place where she could feel safe. Maverick, our rat terrier who we adopted when he was a year and a half old, gave Molly her space too. Since Molly had been a stray picked up on the street, she was clueless about living in a home. Neither jealous nor protective, Maverick soon began to show Molly the ropes. Housebreaking was difficult, but with Maverick as an example, she became a pro. Whatever he did, she would do. Now, in cooler months when Mav puts his sweater on, Molly wants to wear her teal knitted coat too!

Molly • red merle/fox terrier mix • 9½ years old

Molly likes to find low-lying branches in the garden and do a slow-motion walk under them, going back and forth. Our Christmas tree is fair game!

Molly likes to find low-lying branches in the garden and do a slow-motion walk under them, going back and forth. Our Christmas tree is fair game! Another endearing habit is to prance to the back door in the morning.

The dogs are good company. Molly likes to play hide-and-seek with our granddaughter. She's a barker and alerts me to anyone coming to the door or walking on the road. One of Molly's favorite places to sit is outside the back door, where I have placed her dog bed on a table. From this elevated perch, she has a bird's-eye view of the back yard.

When I turn in for the night, the dogs come with me. Molly sleeps on her bed beside mine. After getting up in the morning and doing her daily routine, she will get on the bed and watch me get ready to start the day.

—*Tess Teliska*

MATCHMAKING
TIP

Molly can't replace a former
beloved pet, but with her big
personality, she helps fill the void.

—*Peggy Story Brink*

Gigi

AT HOME WITH PATSY AND PATRICK AELVOET
San Antonio, Texas

Gigi was to have been our neighbor Terri's foster dog. I met her the day she arrived, and when Terri had to leave town that first weekend, Gigi stayed with us. She's still here!

Gigi's favorite ritual, by far, is mealtime. She shows her delight by twirling and twirling! When she arrived, she was emaciated—every rib was clearly visible. She ate as though she was eating her last meal. She still does!

We also noticed that she had bad teeth. And her tail was bleeding from having been repeatedly banged on something. During her first week with us her tail condition worsened and the vet had to crop it. The next week we took her to a canine teeth specialist. He removed some teeth and gave her a root canal. Until then, she had been in a lot of pain.

She also needed a name. I felt that a dog that had been through so much, yet was still so sweet and loving, deserved a famous name. I love the movie *Gigi* with Leslie Caron. So there it was—Gigi!

Gigi looks like an English Lab, and her personality is pure joy. So easy to love, she blended right into our family. She and her new sister Aspen, a purebred lab, immediately became best friends. From the start, she went to bed at 10:00 p.m. in her crate next to Aspen's crate and never whimpered. She did have some accidents, but knowing her past, I couldn't be mad. I was home every day and gave her lots of attention and love. After a few weeks with a diet of grain-free dog food, her dull coat became shiny. Now and then she gets a breakfast taco (eggs and bacon only).

No trainer was necessary for Gigi, as she learned quickly to go potty outside. Now she sits by the door or whines when she needs to go out. And she quickly learned to come when called.

Gigi loves to chase balls, though she doesn't return them. She is quite the adventuress. One night after dinner out, Patrick and I came home and called the dogs in. We noticed a large porcupine half-hiding behind a flower pot. The dogs went right by without disturbing it, and we looked at each other and said, "What good dogs we have." Gigi ran straight to her crate. I followed to say goodnight when I noticed her muzzle was full of porcupine needles. They were also in her mouth! Aspen had them too, although not as many. We set up a little OR with bandages, pliers, water, and antibacterial ointment for dogs and started with Gigi. Very quickly we realized that with a break after every few quills, she was fine with the procedure. But Aspen would have none of it. Both went to the vet the next day.

Gigi is still the sweet girl I met the first day she came to stay with us. She is a lover, not a watchdog. Aspen takes care of security.

—*Patsy Aelvoet*

ADOPTION
TIP

Understand that your dog comes
with baggage and needs lots of love
and patience. It helps to have
someone who will take them out
and play with them or just be there
for love.

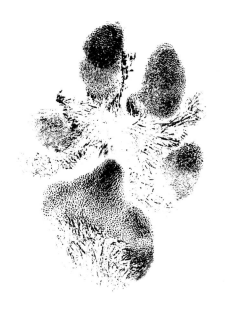

Gigi • Labrador mix • 10 years old

Gigi looks like an English Lab,
and her personality is pure joy. So
easy to love, she blended right
into our family.

MATCHMAKING
TIP

A needy dog must be paired
with a caring person, who
will shower it with TLC!

—Peggy Story Brink

Tater

AT HOME WITH CRUZ HERR
Redmond, Washington

When I was fourteen, I got a Jack Russell terrier puppy that lived with me until he was seventeen years old. Now I was at the airport to greet my first rescue dog. The two-month-old puppy had flown all the way from Texas to Washington State. His name at the adoption facility was Tate. When he arrived, he was much smaller than I expected, weighing in at 8 or 9 pounds—about the size of a russet potato. It was only fitting to call him Tater.

Tater was really scared, and rightfully so. He carefully crawled out of the kennel and got to know me before we ventured to his new home by car. This was just the beginning of a journey where he would hear new noises and experience all sorts of unfamiliar scents.

When Tater arrived home, he was fearful. He explored inside for about thirty minutes before embarking on the great outdoors. He was naturally curious, but hesitant to step foot on unfamiliar surfaces. One surface he got acquainted with was the sun-beaten porch floor, where he warmed right up and instantly claimed for summer naps. His voyage had exhausted

him and created quite the appetite. Every piece of food provided vanished in moments, and I sensed his comfort level rise.

Over time, Tater built confidence. We built trust with each other quickly and he kept me in sight constantly. Tater remains curious but is skeptical of new places and people, which he expresses with an endearing raised eyebrow. He delivers a low, happy grumble accompanied by a forceful tail wag that shakes his entire backside when his favorite people approach. He also tends to lick his people so gently that his tongue carries out only half the motion, leaving his wet tongue stuck on you for seconds at a time. It is an odd quirk but I relish those moments.

From the beginning, Tater has been a loyal companion. He enjoys sitting under my legs, tables, beds, and couches if he can fit. He finds comfort in those tight, secure spaces. Early on he was fond of his oversized kennel that was nestled up to the side of my bed. However, once I allowed him to lie next to me on the bed while I read, there was no turning back. His stays on

my bed grew longer until he was a full-time sleeping buddy hogging my covers every night. His preference is to be under the covers, sprawled out and constantly squirming, which can make for some restless nights, but I wouldn't have it any other way. When Tater isn't sleeping on the bed, he can usually be found curled up on the couch or on one of his two dog beds. When I'm away you can find Tater at the edge of the bed, alertly looking out the window, watching the birds, cars, and people in motion. After getting settled in the evening Tater is quick to find a crevice under your arm or space between your back and the couch cushion, where he will carry on playing with his toys.

When Tater was just a pup, he and I spent a lot of time at off-leash dog parks and wandering the nearby beach. These activities were great for stimulating his mind and developing his social skills. After a few visits to his favorite places he gravitated toward the larger dogs. The bigger breeds seemed to be conscious of his youth and size and played gently with equal amounts of patience.

115

Tater • Staffordshire mix • 15 months old

Tater delivers a low, happy grumble accompanied by a forceful tail wag that shakes his entire backside when his favorite people approach.

I had taken my former dog to obedience training, and I used those principles with Tater. I'm also fortunate that Tater has spent a great deal of time with my girlfriend's mom who owns a dog daycare, BowWow Fun Towne, and is a certified trainer. Through repetition at the parks and at daycare, Tater developed strong recall and communication skills. When Tater has needs, he makes it pretty clear in his own way. If he isn't feeling well or needs to go out, he will mutter or nose me until I get up to assess the situation. Like any dog, when he feels neglected, he'll communicate that, sometimes by destroying something. In classic form, he once chewed up a dress shoe. When I discovered the mauled shoe, he felt so guilty that he crammed his shaking body behind the toilet, making every attempt to avoid eye contact. Once he did look at me, I could see the shame on his face.

Each day Tater greets me with a well of energy, so playtime is something he cherishes. One of Tater's favorite games is wrestling. He loves it when I get down on his level, where he can wildly lick and nibble on my limbs. Occasionally he will get me into a tug-of-war match, and he is undefeated. Tater is not a natural retriever by any means. He'll be happy to chase a ball in motion but lacks any degree of hustle to be competitive with other dogs. A game of fetch usually turns into me doing the fetching; nonetheless, we enjoy the time together. The best decision I have made is to adopt Tater. Throughout the process, I was given ample information that made it much less daunting than I anticipated. I'm a firm advocate of adopting or fostering if the situation is right. There has been nothing more fulfilling than being able to change Tater's life. The bond we've built is truly priceless.

—*Cruz Herr*

ADOPTION
TIP

Find the right age, breed, and
temperament of dog that is
compatible with your family
and living arrangements.

MATCHMAKING
TIP

Cruz's lifestyle is super-energetic. He wanted a companion that would enjoy the outdoors with him. A short-haired, big-breed pup would be the perfect pal. Tater filled the bill!

—*Peggy Story Brink*

122

Ginger and Cheddar

AT HOME WITH ALLAN AND JO SCHMIDT
Fair Oaks Ranch, Texas

Ginger was a stray, according to San Antonio Animal Care Services (ACS). The owners were found, but they rejected her and wouldn't pay the kennel fee. Peggy Story Brink, founder of CARE Animal Rescue, happened to see Ginger the day before she was to be euthanized and pulled her out of the lineup. She was about four years old when we agreed to foster her.

Within two days, we found that she got along well with our other three rescue dogs, so we adopted her. To name her we had only to look at her golden-blonde hair. With a calm, laid-back manner—the sweetest nature of all our dogs—she fit into our family from day one. She just wants to please us.

Two years later, we adopted another rescue, Cheddar. Cheddar's story is more complicated. In February 2013, a woman in Midland, Texas, adopted Cheddar, a one-year-old Border collie mix, from CARE. That April, Peggy got a call from the Midland City kennel director that they had the dog. She learned that the woman first wanted the kennel to keep him for a few weeks, but then asked them to euthanize her.

Peggy put out a call asking if someone could go to Midland to bring her back to San Antonio. On May 9, Allan and his brother-in-law drove 350 miles to Midland, and the next day brought Ginger to San Antonio.

We fostered Cheddar to transition her to a normal life. She was protective of us and got along well with our four other dogs. As has happened to us before when we fostered a dog, we decided to keep Cheddar, who is loving and smart. After a few months we put her in a 24/7 training and evaluation program with Sit Means Sit. She was with a trainer and his family and their dogs for two weeks and responded well to the training. We have wondered what happened in Midland in less than two months to cause the woman to want to kill this beautiful dog. Cheddar is now a significant part of our family.

—*Allan and Jo Schmidt*

124

ADOPTION
TIP

Formal training for the adopted dog
must involve family members who
will observe the training rules.
Otherwise, formal training can be
undone. Add a how to train your
dog book to your home library!

Cheddar • Border collie mix
7 years old

Ginger • Labrador
9 years old

Within two days, we found that Ginger
got along well with our other dogs.
Two years later we adopted Cheddar,
who is loving and smart.

MATCHMAKING
TIP

Ginger, sweet and calm, fit
into the Schmidts' family life
from day one. However,
Cheddar was rambunctious
and had no social skills. Al and
Jo enrolled her in a formal
training program so that she
could learn the household
rules and how to become a
beloved member of their pack.

—*Peggy Story Brink*

Stella

AT HOME WITH TOM, JESSICA, WILL, JACK, AND KAYLA KOZAK
San Antonio, Texas

I have been around dogs for most of my life, but my husband, Tom, had never had a dog and was apprehensive about it. We went to see a fostered dog named Sassy. Completely shaved because her hair had become matted with fleas, she was friendly but a bit standoffish. Nevertheless, Sassy found her way into our hearts. Since Tom was the least enthusiastic, the children and I thought that naming her after something he liked would help. So we named her after Stella beer. As it turned out, he took to Stella right away, and she to him. In that knowing way of dogs, after a while Stella began to gravitate to our son Will, who had shared Tom's hesitation about having a dog.

Stella is walked three times each day: in the morning by Tom or me, at noon by our dog walker Chantal, and in the afternoon by Kayla, Jack, or Will, who take turns. Stella has three beds. In the morning while I'm working out she rests in her bed in the dining room, directly across from our home gym. During the day she naps on a bed nestled under a coffee table in the living room. At night she sleeps in a round, super-comfy bed on the floor of our bedroom.

Each morning Stella wakes up with our alarm and runs around the bed, excited to begin the day—and eat breakfast! In the morning we feed her raw beef sliders for dogs, along with beef broth and goat's milk. In the evening, she gets kangaroo dog food with coconut oil and goat's milk. She loves to eat and would weigh far more than her thirteen pounds if we let her eat whenever she wanted.

Although she is friendly with everyone in the family, Stella identified me as the alpha in our house and stays close. One day when I was organizing a closet, Stella meandered in and stood between my legs as I sat on the floor. When I closed my legs slightly, Stella jumped over my leg and ran away as fast as she could—through the bathroom, into the bedroom, and right back to stand between my legs. Tom and I thought, "Hmm, that's odd." But it turned into a game that went on for quite a while. We could not stop laughing.

138

Early on, Tom raised his voice to scold one of the kids, looked around, and saw that Stella was not in one of her usual spots. We found her hiding, her heart going a mile a minute. She must have thought she was getting yelled at. It is painful to wonder what her life was like before we met her. Stella gets along well with humans but not other dogs. Training has helped, but it's still a challenge. She is also a watch dog—to a point. If she catches the shadow of someone approaching the front door, she goes bananas barking. As soon as the person enters, though, she sniffs them and is excited to be petted and loved.

—*Jessica Kozak*

Stella • mixed poodle, dachshund, Chihuahua • 3½ years old

*Stella thinks she is a large
dog and can go up against
any other dog!*

ADOPTION
TIP

When choosing a dog that fits
your family and lifestyle, be
patient and wait for the right
fit. It's worth it!

MATCHMAKING
TIP

Match an adaptable dog to a
family with children—not a
one-man dog, but one that
gets along with other people.

—*Peggy Story Brink*

Mazie

AT HOME WITH STEVE, FARRELL, AND FRAN MELNICK
West Hempshead, New York

We first met Mazie on FaceTime. She was missing her tail, but we thought she was cute. Mazie arrived at our house after fourteen hours in a crate and a flight delay, pooped in our living room, then followed me right upstairs. We soon bonded and she followed me all over the house.

Mazie never pooped in the house again. She does a great bum wiggle and has beautiful, big brown eyes. Her foster mom calls them soulful; our vet calls them beautiful.

It took Mazie more than a year to allow us to handle her back legs, likely due to previous trauma. Now she even lets me brush her teeth with an electric toothbrush—a skill set I never knew I had.

Mazie used to wake me up in the morning by putting her paws near my head and barking. I've gotten her to stop that. But she still barks a lot—mostly at strangers and relatives. It took her a while to get used to my brother-in-law. She is a great watch dog.

Mazie claimed the couch in the den on the first day she was here. Now she believes that she is queen of the house and is possessive of her couch. She also tried to claim the living room couch, but we convinced her otherwise. We had a trainer briefly, but with the guidance of family members who have a long history with dogs, we began training Mazie ourselves. She was easy to train, except when walking on a leash—then she likes to sniff all over—is she part blood hound?

All of us needed training! We discovered that food is a great motivator. Mazie will sit, stay, lie down, and "give-paw" for a treat. Recently, we started teaching her to jump over an obstacle to get to the treat.

Mazie is highly attuned to kitchen sounds. When my mom starts cutting or chopping vegetables, Mazie rushes in and sits down in front of her, expecting to be fed. An observant Jewish family, when we sit down Friday night at the

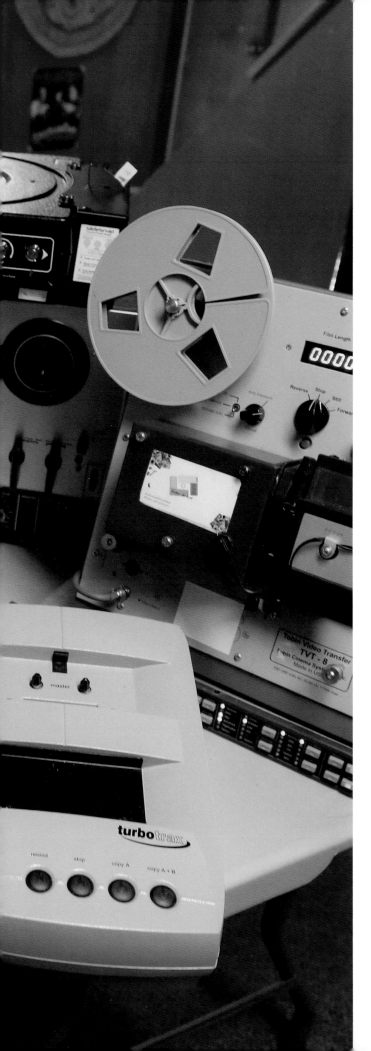

Sabbath meal for which my mom has baked challah, Mazie rushes to the table, sits, and waits for her piece too.

Mazie has her own rain gear, along with a sweater my mom knitted for her. And of course there's the "thunder jacket" she wears during storms.

We have always known that Mazie loves us. When we are happy, she is happy; when someone is sad, she senses it and seems sad. She is very much a one-family and even a one-person (me) dog. Especially endearing is the way she jumps on me and wiggles her bum when I come in the door after a long day at the office. Sometimes she even goes to work with me.

I thank all who have helped us work with Mazie: Peggy Story Brink of CARE-TX, foster mom Teresa Strizich, Rich Laws, Michael and Becky Melnick for medical advice and training, and our great vet, Harry Penson. We thank God for Mazie; we think perhaps God gives us pets to make us better people. If we can care for and love our Mazie, we can do the same for other people.

—*Steve Melnick*

Mazie • schnauzer mix • 6 years old

All of us needed training!
We discovered that food is
a great motivator.

ADOPTION
TIP

Tell your mom you are
looking for a small dog and
adjust the definition of small.
Be patient and provide lots of
positive reinforcement. Your
dog will learn to trust and
love you.

MATCHMAKING
TIP

Fluffy dogs require a
commitment to regular
grooming. Mazie did not like
being groomed, but the
Melnicks worked through
this challenge with patience
and ingenuity.

—*Peggy Story Brink*

Bella Bleu

AT HOME WITH ROB, LORRIE, COLTON, AVERY, AND EMILY CHESHIER
San Antonio, Texas

While walking his dog, a good friend of ours ran into a neighbor who was fostering a dog. He called to say that we should come see the puppy. (Our last child had recently left for college, and I think he was worried we'd be lonely.)

We fell in love with Bella's gentle demeanor. Within ten minutes, we called to say we wanted to adopt her. We filled out the paperwork online that night, were accepted, and picked her up the next day. Although CARE said her name was Adrena, the foster family had named her Bella. We decided to stick with that name, adding the middle name Bleu. Bella Bleu fits her perfectly!

Bella is one of the sweetest dogs we've ever been around. She carries her bone from room to room through the house, like it's her best friend. If I give her a new bone, she always goes back to the same old bone.

Bella is fond of fetching a ball, but she hasn't learned how to drop it when she brings it back. We're working on that. We trained her ourselves because we enjoy spending time with her. Right now she can sit, shake, lay, stay, and *eat.*

Our son in college has a dog similar in size to Bella. When he comes home, he brings Bingo along, and Bingo and Bella have become fast friends. While Bingo loves to swim in the pool, Bella will go to the first step and lie down to get good and wet. Then they shake water everywhere and chase each other through the yard.

Bella climbs up in bed with us for wind-down time before going to sleep in her kennel in our room. We leave the kennel door open, and it's the place she likes to sleep.

Because we live on twenty-five acres, she has lots of room to run, although she doesn't like leaving the fenced yard. She sees deer in the morning and evening but doesn't bark at them. She will bark if a stranger comes close, but it only takes her a minute to befriend any stranger.

Bella is a good companion. We have three children and three grandchildren, and Bella is far easier to manage!

—*Lorrie Cheshier*

ADOPTION
TIP

Dogs need exercise which
alleviates many behavioral
problems. Find an area
where the dog can run free if
at all possible. If it must be
on a leash, get a long one
that will allow him to run
around in the yard or a park.

Bella Bleu • Labrador mix • Less than 1 year old

Bella carries her bone from room to room through the house, like it's her best friend. If I give her a new bone, she always goes back to the same old bone.

170

 ## MATCHMAKING *TIP*

Bella Bleu likes both people
and dogs—a perfect match
for Rob and Lorrie.

—*Peggy Story Brink*

Zeus

AT HOME WITH SCOTT, FELISE, WYATT, AND GARRETT LENGER
Fair Oaks Ranch, Texas

We had a thirteen-year-old Australian shepherd rescue named Bear. Every time someone came over with a dog, or we found a lost dog, Bear would whimper when the dog went home. So we decided to adopt a dog for Bear to play with. When Zeus's foster mom brought him over for a visit, he immediately peed on the Christmas tree and presents before chasing one of our cats. I opened the back door to let him out before he peed on anything else, and he promptly jumped into the pool. When we let him back in the house, he ran to the master bedroom and pooped on the carpet! Much to my husband's chagrin, the rest of us decided we loved him and bade farewell to the foster mom. We now had a big, hairy, orange hot mess of a dog on our hands. His name had been Isaac, then Wolfie, but my son, Garrett, changed his name to Zeus after a dog he saw in a YouTube video. He is now Zeus Wolfie Lenger—nicknamed Trump and Derp.

A sweet and loving dog from the outset, Zeus is still sweet and loving. And he still chases cats but would never eat or harm one. We had an old cat that put him in his place, so he doesn't bother the cats as much now. He enjoys sleeping on the staircase, blocking the cats from going up or down. He also likes to sleep outside my husband's study, and when I'm in the kitchen, he naps there—usually in my way!

Zeus destroyed our patio furniture. He nibbled on Persian carpets, antique wooden furniture, and a few pair of shoes. He thinks the Natuzzi sofa is a dog bed purchased expressly for him. He mostly comes when called, and since day one he has never peed or pooped anywhere but outside. He asks to go out by finding one of us and turning in little circles. We taught him not to beg at the table and are still working on teaching him not to jump up on guests.

Everyone who meets Zeus loves him. He's a sweet, gentle, and silly dog—sometimes just looking at him cracks us up. He's a bit of an escape artist. We need to get a quick handle on him when we open the front door, so he wears a martingale (limited slip) collar. He only barks if he sees someone walking a dog. He wants to play! Garrett likes to play tug with Zeus. Usually that means Garrett holding on to a rope toy and Zeus pulling Garrett all over the house. Zeus's favorite game is a tug-of-war with Bear. They also mock-fight over a blue rubber chicken, and Zeus likes to steal Bear's squeaky pig toy. Zeus loves it when Wyatt and Garrett chase him through the house, pretending to be after his toy.

On CARE's Facebook page we spotted a dog named Vaughn living in Portland, Oregon, that we were certain was Zeus's brother. I reached out to Vaughn's owner and learned that our pups were adopted through CARE within days of each other. They look almost identical and have many of the same mannerisms. When Vaughn's family was in Texas recently, they made an hour-and-a-half drive to meet Zeus. We are even more convinced that Vaughn and Zeus are "brudders" from the same litter.

—*Felise Lenger*

ADOPTION
TIP

Give the dog a chance. We easily could have said "take him back" after he misbehaved on the first visit, but first impressions aren't always accurate, especially with rescue dogs. Were they abused or neglected? Did they wonder if they would ever eat again? Are they worried that they will be left alone again? It is up to us to show the dog that it is cherished and part of a family, and that doesn't happen overnight.

Zeus • goberian (Siberian husky/golden retriever mix) • 4 years old

Zeus thinks the Natuzzi
sofa is a dog bed purchased
expressly for him.

MATCHMAKING
TIP

Small children make some small breeds nervous. Larger breeds such as Labradors and golden retrievers have a temperament wonderfully suited to younger kids. Zeus was just right for the Lenger family.

—*Peggy Story Brink*

Odin

AT HOME WITH DAVID, AMANDA, CARTER, AND ADDISON PALLUCH
Boerne, Texas

Ruby, our seven year-old terrier/pharaoh hound, was apprehensive when we brought a puppy home to foster for CARE. But over the summer we had lost our dog Watson and longed for another one. The puppy was super-sweet and had many mannerisms similar to Watson's. Soon Ruby—who had been best friends with Watson and had become dispirited after his death—found room in her heart for the puppy. We noticed new spunk in Ruby's step—she became more active and played with the puppy. Now they play together for hours at a time and delight in tug-of-war.

Our children, Addison and Carter, have an interest in mythology. So we named the puppy Odin for the Norse God of wisdom, poetry, war, death, divination, and magic, and Watson in honor of the dog we had lost. He became formally Odin Watson and informally Odin.

The early weeks with Odin were both tiring and fun. You forget what it's like getting up all hours of the night with a puppy, but we wouldn't have traded it for the world. We've had him for only a few months and are working on house-training and teaching him to sit. He walks nicely on his leash and likes his reflective collar, which he needs because his coat is so dark that he's hard to see outside.

Odin is sweet, chill, and endearingly clumsy. He loves to chase things but often loses sight of what's around him. He is constantly tipping over or bumping into things in the cutest puppy way. We love his clumsiness—and his love of snuggling.

Odin loves to snuggle. He has his own beds, but he usually prefers to sleep wherever his humans are. If we are in the family room, he will sleep next to us on the couch, his favorite spot.

Odin is our third rescue dog, and we cannot imagine life without one. A rescue's outlook and appreciation of everything is just different. We once had a purebred weimaraner that we loved greatly. However, I don't think we would have anything other than a rescue again.

—*Amanda Palluch*

ADOPTION
TIP

Whether a puppy or an adult, it takes time for a rescue dog to find a routine, but stick with it. The dog will become the most loyal, amazing part of your family.

Odin Watson • spaniel mix • 4 months

Odin is constantly tipping
over or bumping into things
in the cutest puppy way. We
love his clumsiness—and his
love of snuggling.

Dogs are puppies for only a short time before adolescence sets in, with chewing and high energy. Amanda and Chip knew what to expect when their pup was fully grown.

—*Peggy Story Brink*

Peggy Story Brink

In 2009, my husband, Lloyd, and I founded Cressie Animal Refuge and Enrichment (CARE), based in San Antonio, Texas. We had enjoyed rewarding business careers but were inspired to start CARE through a deep love of dogs and a commitment to make a change that would prevent dogs from losing their lives in the shelter system. CARE started as a grassroots effort supported by family, friends, and a tight circle of business associates. That first year we were able to save 171 dogs.

Since 2015, we have expanded into eight markets in the US and Canada. Today, CARE saves more than 650 lives each year. We are committed to the utmost well-being of our dogs. After leaving the shelter and entering our program, they are placed in a foster home, allowing the dogs to be cleared of any health issues and receive veterinary care. Additionally, at this time we are able to assess and correct any basic behavioral concerns. Importantly, this time allows the dog an opportunity to come out of its shell and show its true personality. This prepares them for their new home and gives the adopter the most accurate information before commiting.

Our staff is all about making the perfect match between dogs and their forever families. We value respect and transparency. Potential owners receive all the information needed to make an informed decision. Our staff, corporate sponsors, and board of directors encourage CARE to use the latest technology including social media, FaceTime, videos, and Google Earth to help ensure an appropriate match. We are mindful of the adopter's lifestyle, and these communications platforms allow us to conduct a virtual on-site interview and screening process. This technology offers a thorough yet simple adoption process.

Our staff members, Jessy Gillette and Emily Cleveland, work long hours and manage the many details necessary to assure the quality and health of our animals. They deserve thanks. A special thank you goes to our transport team who work crazy hours securing the safe travel of our dogs to their new homes. Lloyd and I are grateful for the board of directors whose vision has helped guide the organization to be ever more successful. We thank our many event sponsors and foster families who play a key role in our continued growth. And we thank in advance those who will become dog rescuers.

—*Peggy Story Brink*

Jason Oliver Nixon

Jason Oliver Nixon and John Loecke are the duo behind the North Carolina–based interior design and product development firm Madcap Cottage. Known for their whimsical use of color and pattern, the Madcap gents—along with their pound-rescue posse, Weenie, Amy Petunia, and Cecil—scour the world for eclectic finds that capture their unique and gimlet-eyed viewpoint. Imagine a British country house that pairs stunning antiques and a spirited dash of Chinoiserie chic with a dash of Morocco-meets-India élan. Shake, stir, then pour.

Find the Madcap Cottage–curated selection of vintage and antique finds on One Kings Lane and Chairish. The Madcaps have a bestselling fabric collection with Robert Allen @Home and licensed programs with Smith + Noble, York Wallcoverings, BBJ Linen, Mirth Studio, Momeni, Newport Cottages, and Port 68. The Madcaps' latest book is *Prints Charming: Create Absolutely Beautiful Interiors with Prints & Patterns* (Abrams, 2017).

Their work has appeared in the media domestically and internationally in publications such as *InStyle*, *People*, *House Beautiful*, *Country Living*, *Coastal Living*, *House & Garden UK*, *Architectural Digest Russia*, the *New York Times*, the *Wall Street Journal*, and *New York* magazine, among many others.

Afterword

As the author of many books on interior design, it seemed only natural to follow them with a book about how dogs contribute to our sense of home. It's a subject I understand on a personal level too. When our daughter Elizabeth became ill and had to be home-schooled for several months, we thought a dog would be excellent company. She chose an Afghan hound, a descendent of a Westminster Kennel Dog Show winner. TajMa (Harmony's TajMa Khan) was an elegant clown. She was happiest running circles around the neighbors' dogs. She gleefully left them bewildered when she leapt over them in a long, graceful arc, her silky blonde hair streaming in her wake. I miss her comic charm, playfulness, and undemanding love.

TajMa was not a rescue, but some purebreds are. Attorney and noted fashion blogger Jody Spangler DeFord (Red's Shoe Diaries, www.rs-diaries.com) was mom to two Hungarian vizslas, Tim Riggins and Dillon, when the breeder called to ask her and her husband Kevin to foster a third, Kaiser. They agreed. "Of course," she said, "he stole our hearts and Kaiser had a forever home!"

Like their mom, Jody's four-legged pals love to dress up. They even represent the luxury pet accessories brand Three Wags (www.threewags.com), maker of glam neckwear. And the three have their own Instagram site (@timriggins-thevizsla). These three elegant pointers have 12,000 regular followers and about 100 new followers are added weekly.

I agree with Silvia Allen, owner of Sir Freckles (chapter 2), that all dogs need a purpose—and a reward for a job well done. While working as a magazine editor in New York City, I was scouting the New Jersey home of Yogi Berra for a kitchen remodeling story. While we were talking, two carpenters working in the basement started up the stairs on their way outside. When the Berras' German shepherd heard their footsteps, he began a low, ominous growl. It continued as the men passed, with the dog at their heels all the way to the door. Once they were outside, the dog returned to me, lifted his head and looked at me, waiting for acknowledgment of a job well done. "Good dog, great job!" I said, patting him. He nodded, walked to the door and laid down—keeping vigilant watch for those two

Jody Spanger DeFord with her rescued vizslas, Tim Riggins and Kaiser. Kaiser gives Jody a kiss.

potential troublemakers to return.

When I took a job as director of interior design for a New York City music distributor and was sent to Florida to design its new 244,000-square-foot headquarters, I continued working with private interior-design clients. Sam and Doug, rescues belonging to client-friends Stephanie and Richard Stern, looked like the black and white Scotties on the Dewars whiskey package. What struck me was their relationship—Sam the general, Doug his able aide-de-camp, always looking to Sam for direction. During one summer, on Fridays I would fly from Palm Beach to New York City and drive with the Sterns to their Massachusetts cottage to check on their addition, a sixteenth-century English barn. One Friday I arrived before noon to hear that the Sterns couldn't leave the city until Saturday

morning. I offered to drive Sam and Doug to the cottage where they could run free on the large lawn. That night my two companions outdid themselves as watchdogs. Sam ran from window to window, Doug at his heels, barking furiously at every squirrel, skunk, rabbit, and deer that came by. Around 4:30 a.m., desperate for sleep, I called ringleader General Sam and threatened him. "Sam, if you bark one more time, I am jailing you in the cellar." I tell you truthfully, he understood every word! And he gave orders to Doug—no more watchdogging.

Here in San Antonio, Emily Spicer often posts on Facebook about her rescues, Dobson and Sebastian. I believe that at times they are taste testers for recipes she creates as food editor of the *San Antonio Express-News*. We know that if Dobson and Sebastian like it, readers of her

Emily Spicer, features editor and food editor at the *San Antonio Express-News*, often updates fans of Dobson and Sebastian on Facebook.

"Emily's Easy Entertaining" column will love it!

These and other dogs are frequently on my mind and forever in my heart. It is easy to see why the featured rescuers who have shared their stories speak so touchingly of their dogs' love and of their love for these marvelous creatures. Thank you, Peggy Story Brink and CARE, for caring. Thank you, Jason Oliver Nixon, owner of four rescues, for a charming foreword, a tribute to Jasper. Thank you, Natalia, for your wonderful photography. And thanks for suggesting that we coauthor this book—a work of love.

—*Patricia Hart McMillan*

Peggy Story Brink and Arree.

Natalia King-Sun crisscrosses the United States in her work as a commercial photographer. At home in San Antonio, Texas, she maintains a studio specializing in portraiture of people and their pets. Natalia holds a BA in art history and an MA in education from the Daugavpils Pedagogical University in Latvia, her native country. She earned a degree in graphic design from the Art Institute in Fort Lauderdale, Florida. To see more of Natalia's work, visit www.nataliasun.com.

Patricia Hart McMillan has degrees in English literature, art history, and interior design and has worked as a magazine editor, writer, and interior designer. Her interior designs have been published in leading magazines such as *House Beautiful, The Designer, Ladies Home Journal*, and *Woman's Day*, and in newspapers including *USA Today, Parade*, and the *New York Times*. Pat, who has authored 22 books on interior design and architecture, is best known for *Home Decorating for Dummies. At Home with Dogs* is her first book about man's best friend.